BLUE-COLLAR ENLIGHTENMENT

A Guide to an Awakened Consciousness for Ordinary People

MIKAL SHUMATE

BALBOA.PRESS
A DIVISION OF HAY HOUSE

Copyright © 2020 Mikal Shumate.

All rights reserved. No part of this book may be used or reproduced by any means, graphic, electronic, or mechanical, including photocopying, recording, taping or by any information storage retrieval system without the written permission of the author except in the case of brief quotations embodied in critical articles and reviews.

Balboa Press books may be ordered through booksellers or by contacting:

Balboa Press
A Division of Hay House
1663 Liberty Drive
Bloomington, IN 47403
www.balboapress.com
1 (877) 407-4847

Because of the dynamic nature of the Internet, any web addresses or links contained in this book may have changed since publication and may no longer be valid. The views expressed in this work are solely those of the author and do not necessarily reflect the views of the publisher, and the publisher hereby disclaims any responsibility for them.

The author of this book does not dispense medical advice or prescribe the use of any technique as a form of treatment for physical, emotional, or medical problems without the advice of a physician, either directly or indirectly. The intent of the author is only to offer information of a general nature to help you in your quest for emotional and spiritual well-being. In the event you use any of the information in this book for yourself, which is your constitutional right, the author and the publisher assume no responsibility for your actions.

Any people depicted in stock imagery provided by Getty Images are models, and such images are being used for illustrative purposes only.
Certain stock imagery © Getty Images.

Print information available on the last page.

ISBN: 978-1-9822-4433-0 (sc)
ISBN: 978-1-9822-4435-4 (hc)
ISBN: 978-1-9822-4434-7 (e)

Library of Congress Control Number: 2020910445

Balboa Press rev. date: 06/03/2020

Content is light encoded to assist your journey.

CONTENTS

Preface ix

Acknowledgment xi

Introduction xiii

Chapter 1   Awakened vs. Enlightened 1

Chapter 2   Consciousness Is Self-Awareness......................................7

Chapter 3   You Are *Not* Your Body!..13

Chapter 4   You Are *Not* Your Mind!...17

Chapter 5   You *Are* Your Soul, Spirit, Higher Self..........................31

Chapter 6   Stress! 35

Chapter 7   Fear 41

Chapter 8   The Road to Awakening and Enlightenment................47

Chapter 9   Advanced Spiritual Theories...55

Chapter 10 My Story..65

PREFACE

I claim no original authorship of the materials presented herein. Rather, I have taken a lifetime of study from many and varied sources on the topic of consciousness and spirituality and condensed them into simplified terms in a way that almost everyone can understand. With that comes the opportunity for everyone to improve his or her experience of life to be happy, to live in abundance and free of stress.

—Mikal

ACKNOWLEDGMENT

Many thanks to the insights that provided clarity and organization for the book structure from my friend Bob Barr, whom I met while walking my dogs years before I wrote the book. Who would have known then that this friendship would play a major role in helping me get this book published in a form that makes sense? Thanks, Bob!

INTRODUCTION

Consciousness has no religion, no belief or ideology, no gender, no sexuality, no race, no age, and no nationality. Consciousness is none of these things yet is experiencing all these things.

You are consciousness - Nassim Haramein

Awakening Is the Door to Enlightenment

Who doesn't want love in their life, to be happy, to not have to struggle with life or to suffer with their existence? To transcend our normal state of existence requires a higher state of consciousness, and I am going to explain how to achieve this for those who know little about it, blue-collar folks. It is my intention to distill complex spiritual concepts into easy-to-understand language, with the goal of realizing the essence of a process that improves one's experience of life. This is not a belief system; it is an experience or state of being achievable by all who are willing to do the work.

Unless you are one of the few and the fortunate, your life hasn't been joyful except in spurts, just enough to know what's missing most of the time. We live our lives stressed by something, be it basic survival or the struggle for fulfillment of our desires. Whether it's coping with our relationships, making enough money, or being conflicted about what we want and what we *should* or *deserve* to get or anywhere in between, we have built-in obstacles that impede our success. Even those with the proverbial silver spoon have their share of problems. It is the way of life, but it doesn't have to remain that way. There is a simple way to break out of this cycle of suffering and into a state of happiness, joy, and abundance that is possible to achieve in this lifetime.

Can you even imagine such a state of existence? Can you even begin to dream of living your life with joy as the underlying basis of how you feel *everything*? I mean, to tangibly feel a state of love, magnified exponentially to that of joy, which lies right at the surface of your senses. You can almost touch it, but you certainly can feel it as the state of your existence. Free of the incessant chitter-chatter of the mind, being and experiencing life moment to moment, knowing what is needed in that moment instead of thinking what might be needed or worrying about what was needed in the past? Having the sense that all you need is provided and that the path is before you, and you are guided, mysteriously, along that path. Having the sense that somehow you are connected to everyone and everything in creation, that we are all *one*. Beyond imagination? Perhaps, but this *is* the way humankind is intended to be; it *is* the way we are intended to live.

This is actually a simple thing in and of itself, yet it is a most difficult thing to achieve because so many obstacles are placed in our path. We all have some baggage to carry (unresolved issues of an emotional nature that are detrimental to us). Some of us spend our lifetimes shedding as much baggage as possible, while others continuously add baggage until the weight becomes unbearable. Most are somewhere in between. This is suffering. This need not be the way of life, but we are caught up in our circumstances and can't see the way out. The mind continuously reminds us of the things that bother us most. *Why?* Why do we revisit past traumas, mire in past events, pine for something to come in the future? Because that is the way the mind is, and when we let it rule us, it leads us into a suffering state.

Where do we experience suffering? In the *body,* that's where. No matter what the source of our pain—physical, psychological, or existential—we experience it in the body, be it physical ailments, disease, anxiety, stress, sadness, grief, or loneliness. All are relatable to sensations in the body. All suffering manifests in some way in the body and is most often triggered by *thoughts.* Even so-called accidents are most often caused by being in a distracted state, thinking about something rather than being totally present for the moment, thus missing the cues that could prevent or mitigate something adverse from happening to us. Then sometimes it's just fate.

Krishnaji, one of my teachers, said, "There are only two states of being, a stressed or suffering state and a beautiful state.[1] We all can relate to a stressed state. Anytime you are running through or preoccupied with thoughts from your past (memories) that are disturbing you; anytime you are jacked up because something isn't the way you want it or think it should be; anytime you are anticipating what might happen and have anxiety, fear, dread, or the myriad of negative emotions when looking to the future, you are in a stressful state. When you are in the *now* moment and are able to face the world as it actually is, you are in a beautiful state. If you fully experience your life, there is no residue, nothing left over to hang on to and get tucked away for the future. When you are in that beautiful state, there is peace, appreciation, gratitude, love, and joy. So, the question is, why aren't we there?

To answer that question, we need to recognize how we are manipulated by our minds and egos. We do not experience actual reality, because our minds are constantly interfering. They distract us from being in the now moment of our experience by bringing up things from the past or fears of what might be in the future. Have you ever noticed, while listening to someone speaking, how your mind drifts onto other thoughts, and you actually miss parts of what is being said?

---

[1] From "The Four Sacred Secrets: For Love and Prosperity, A Guide to Living in a Beautiful State" by Preethaji and Krishnaji, available on Amazon.

In reality, which is the now moment of our experience, there can be no room for suffering, because you are fully experiencing what is going on at the time. No matter what your reaction is to the circumstance of the moment, if you fully experience it, there is no residue. Negative emotions are triggered by memories of similar situations or conflictual conditioning, which cause you to feel the same emotional response as the core incident. You cannot help it, and most people have no control over it. For example, you get angry when someone cuts you off in traffic. That surge of emotions is so immediate and instantaneous, it just happens. You hardly have time to recognize the thought that precipitated it. That moment becomes your frame of experience. Your mind interferes by criticizing, commenting, condemning, and comparing yesterday with today and tomorrow. Mind is nothing but the flow of thought. When you are drinking a cup of coffee, are you fully attentive to the experience of the smell, taste, and temperature of the coffee—or are your thoughts on what you're going to do today, what's the score, or how's the market doing, or some other distraction that takes you away from the experience of the moment?

One of the things that is clear about life is that we all have our own idea of what is right and what should be. We all filter the events of the world through the structure we have set up for ourselves, based upon programming and conditioning that is unique to each person.

There is enough similarity within societies that mutual goals can be exercised for the perceived common good, but within those societies is still a broad diversity of thought. The smaller the group, the closer the similarity of goals or views of the world. All this is held in the context of survival—not just physical survival, but the survival of your ego identity and beliefs. People band together out of mutual interest because it increases the chance for survival. To overcome mere survival and to grow as conscious beings, we must recognize these patterns of personal and social conditioning and how the mind uses these to manipulate us. The biggest obstacle to higher consciousness is breaking free of the programming and conditioning that dictates our thinking. We must understand why we think the way we think. To do this requires *awareness.*

Awareness begins with the simple observation of your world, filtered through the mechanism of your thoughts. When you practice just observing or *seeing* the thoughts that pop into your head, sooner or later you will come to the conclusion that you have no explanation why certain thoughts arise. Have you ever said to yourself, "I wonder where that thought came from?" Sometimes bizarre things come to mind that seem totally disconnected from your present circumstance, things that make no sense. This is so because you are not the creator of your thoughts but are rather the attractor of thoughts. They do not come from your mind; instead, they come *through* your mind. This is perhaps the first great revelation on the path to higher consciousness. To understand this concept, Carl Jung was the first Westerner to address the idea of the collective unconscious, where the unconscious mind is shared among beings of the same species. According to Jung, the human collective unconscious is populated by instincts, architypes, and symbols. This concept is addressed as the *thought sphere* in Eastern mystical teachings, which holds that the human mind is millions of years old, and all thoughts that have ever existed reside in that thought sphere. The brain does not hold thoughts; it holds the emotional memory of experiences and events in the form of electrical signals and impulses about things that have already occurred, whether in the short or long term. All is memory. When something in our environment triggers a memory, we remember it as feelings that attract thoughts about those feelings. Thoughts are the symbolic reconstruction of the memory. As soon as an experience passes the *now moment,* it becomes history and memory of that experience.

Thoughts can be constructive or disruptive. An example of constructive thinking would be creativity, analysis and problem solving, insight and awareness. Disruptive thinking is random and unfocused thoughts, indulgence, or obsession in the memory of past events, especially those with an emotional component. Self-obsession, self-judgment, and wishful thinking are a few examples. Have you ever wondered about how some people can come up with the ideas they do? How do artists envision their art, writers construct their novels, and architects design their buildings? Where does creativity come from? Or the ideas that form when problem solving and figuring something out? Part of that has to do with the physical structure of the brain itself on an individual basis, and part has to do with tapping into that collective mind, where all thoughts and ideas exist. We label this *intelligence,* and on the grand scale *divine intelligence,* from which all things are created. The normal process of the mind is to respond or engage with thoughts as they arise. Thoughts arise from what we perceive, which can be through any of the five senses. All this information is filtered through the lower "survival" brain *first,* to check if what we are perceiving is a threat. Any memory we have that remotely relates to that instant perception gets triggered as if that memory were the now situation. So, when a trigger arises, bringing the thought and feeling of a memory, you automatically start following that story, often retelling or replaying it again and again.

To reach an awakened state of consciousness, you must develop a practice of seeing your thoughts before you engage in those thoughts. Once you start observing your thoughts, you can proceed to the next stage, which is tracking your thoughts to determine the source of meaning or the *core* experience for that thought. All meaning is taken from the decisions and conclusions we make that create structure for the life we live. For example, as children, we are playing in the park when suddenly, a dog runs up and jumps on us, both startling us and pushing us to the ground, causing us to bump our heads. Now, the dog may not have meant any harm and just had a habit of jumping up as a friendly gesture and means of getting attention, but to our young selves, it was not a pleasant experience. Thereafter, when we were around dogs, we became frightful and developed a phobia or fear about dogs. In the process of awareness, what is important is understanding what we have created as value and meaning filters by which we see the events of our lives and choose our positions or *stands*. (To stand is to put our foot down and stubbornly hold our position.) Much of what we stand for is constructive and beneficial; some of those stands are created out of survival mind and no longer serve us as we mature and develop higher states of consciousness. Holding firm to stands that no longer serve us is one of the largest obstacles to higher consciousness and enlightenment. The willingness to look at all the things that create our view of the world is the mark of a true warrior, because it is not easy to revisit so many things in our past that hold negative emotional content. However, the easiest way to do this is simply to observe your thoughts. It is those thoughts that relate to disruptive memories of past traumas that are most significant. They are the most likely to keep us trapped in our past suffering, which creates stress. Such is the case where the fear of dogs might have been perceived as a protective mechanism as a child but keeps us paralyzed as an adult. Yet this no longer is a needed survival mechanism. It simply creates stress around dogs when no threat exists.

"Reality" is what we take to be true. What we take to be true is what we believe. What we believe is based upon our perceptions. What we perceive depends upon what we look for. What we look for depends upon what we think. What we think depends upon what we perceive. What we perceive depends upon what we believe. What we believe determines what we take to be true. What we take to be true is our reality.[2]

---

[2] *The Dancing Wu Li Masters* by Gary Zukav, page 344

CHAPTER 1

Awakened vs. Enlightened

You don't have to be a spiritual or religious person to have an awakened consciousness or to be enlightened.

Awaken: To become aware of what is really true or real.[3]

Enlightenment: More than just the simple belief that divinity lies within all life equally, it is the personal experience of this; Your inner state of being that was present as young a child but lost around the age of 2 or 3, that inner quality found joy from within, laughed endlessly, and had wondered in awe of the world; no worries or burden carried around as a result of the passage of time; can be measured by the depth and degree of inner peace.[4]

What is an awakened consciousness, and why would I want one? The obvious answer might be that an awakened consciousness is some

---

[3] Urban Dictionary by Working2OpenUrMind&Heart February 02, 2011

[4] Urban Dictionary by ClosertoNature April 27, 2011

kind of a state of mind, but it is not. It's a state of pure awareness, knowing. To understand this, we need to understand how the process of life works on this planet. We also to need expand our view of life beyond the programming we received as we grew up, because that's where the difficulty starts. The movement toward a higher consciousness is a natural evolutionary process, and the awakening of the awareness to this process is like the opening of a door to a higher self. It is the point where the ordinary consciousness realizes that it is more than the body or the mind. Awakening is the first rung of the ladder of a continuing and almost never-ending process of the expansion of awareness and consciousness. Sooner or later, everyone will experience this awakening of awareness, because that is the natural path of existence.

Awakening consciousness is a process, not a thing. It is not a dogma, philosophy, or code of conduct. It is about being aware of the process of existence, and in so doing, it leads to higher states of consciousness, enlightenment, and ultimately, God realization. To explain a little further, there are three significant milestones on the spiritual path, which is what the quest for enlightenment is, a path to an enriched consciousness that brings a fuller experience of life. That first step, as has been explained, is awakening. Awakening is a threshold that, once crossed, opens your awareness to the fact that we are neither our bodies nor our minds. Once experienced, this realization is irreversible. Once you have crossed it, you cannot go back into the veil of ignorance. You may allow your survivalist mind to presage ignorance temporarily, but once crossed, the imprint of truth resides under the surface and will arise again at some point. Enlightenment has a number of characteristics, the most significant being that of presence, or being in the *now* moment. This is experienced as the amount of time spent in the now or present moment. This is what we are after, because the predominant quality of being in the now is inner peace and freedom from stress. The goal for most people is to be in that higher state around 70 to 80 percent of the time. God realization is a state of cosmic consciousness, where the "*I*" becomes *we* and the individual self realizes its inseparability from the cosmic self, or the ever-expanding universal self. It is a state of consciousness where you are both the form and the formless; you are all existence and beyond all existence.

Our goal in this work is to put you on a path to achieving an enlightened consciousness. Once there, you will know what to do. At this moment, there is actually nothing to do—nothing to be except aware of whatever is there for you in this moment. Being in the moment connects you with the flow of life. It disconnects you from the clutter and chitchat of the mind, leaving you to experience what is actually there instead of living in fear of what might be or remaining attached to what has already been. To do so is to live life completely free. That is what we want!

The path of awakened consciousness is different from the path of religious traditions. It is an inward journey to and beyond the core of the self, to the essence of our being, our god-self. Religious tradition is about faith and the rules of behavior dictated by that faith. Religion is also about being right and righteous in the belief that your god is the right god and the view all others hold of God is incorrect and inferior to yours. Just look at all the wars that have been fought over whose view of God is right and all the atrocities that have been perpetrated in the name of a belief. Awakened consciousness recognizes the god within all beings. Religion is about how to act in the world as interpreted by whichever prophet set down the rules and the philosophy of that tradition. All religious tradition has value as the basis for morality, without which humanity could not have begun to be civilized. The problem with all religions is that they exist for the survival of the organization, even at the expense of the people they are purported to serve. Awakened consciousness does not recognize these artificially created barriers that create separation within humanity. It sees that we are all connected. We see how this separation occurs and what is to be done to move beyond separation into a unified consciousness, at one with all. We look at human suffering, which is created by the illusion of separation, and see how an awakened consciousness can be a path to the alleviation of this suffering.

All human beings deserve to be happy and totally fulfilled in their lives, to have love and joy as the basis for their existence, to be totally free of suffering, fear, anxiety, pain, and lack of anything their hearts truly desire that does not conflict with or impinge upon the free will of another. The following chapters will tell you how the system of life works and discuss the obstacles to achieve that idyllic life. I'll tell you how to manifest all your heart desires. Finally, I'll give you tools to use to become awakened and show you where you go from there.

CHAPTER 2

Consciousness Is Self-Awareness

Understanding this is the key to living a life with purpose and meaning. Awareness is everything! Have you ever wondered, *What is the purpose of life?* I contend that it is all about knowing oneself, which is achieved through awareness. The very first step to self-awareness is knowing how we know what we know and believe what we believe. It's about how our minds work.

> A rational mind, based upon the impressions that it receives from its limited perspective, forms structures which thereafter determine what it further will or will not accept freely. From that point on, regardless of how the real world actually operates, this rational mind, following its self-imposed rules, tries to superimpose on the real world its own version of what must be.[5]

What this is saying is that through our experiences in life from the earliest age, we create our own versions of reality. Once that version sets, it is difficult to see that it might need to be revised, even in the face of contradictory reality. We create our own meanings and seek others

---

[5] *The Dancing Wu Li Masters* by Gary Zukav, page 179

who share that meaning to reinforce that we are right. The mind always wants to be right, which is why it is so difficult to correct the perception and see what is actually real. It is even more difficult when what we believe is connected to things that cannot be scientifically proven, such as religious beliefs. The mind thrives on the belief that what it perceives is correct and necessary to be safe, to survive, and to get what it wants. So, the first step toward enlightenment starts with self-awareness of your own ego, that creation of the mind that is labeled *you*.

How does your mind work? What are your value perceptions? How were you raised, and what are your beliefs? Once you see these things, you then need to become aware of what trauma you carry from the lesson-learning processes that formed those values. This is an extremely difficult process, because while you are examining those values, you are also living them and reliving those things that have pain associated with them. We tend to repress anything that is painful, so digging up those events does not come naturally, even though these can often be the driving events of our lives. Every time you reveal a core value and how you got it, you expand your awareness. The expansion of consciousness is the result of increased awareness. As this process proceeds, your field of awareness and consciousness expands. This expansion is actually a pathway to higher consciousness where, at some point, you reach a step on the ladder called *enlightenment*. There are many steps on this ladder, but it really is possible to reach enlightenment, although the path is fraught with difficulties that are largely of our own creation.

The Secret

I'm going to let you in on a secret, or what was once called a secret, which really wasn't a secret—it was just something that was difficult to understand. What is hidden from the mind and is therefore unknown has that quality of mystery and secrecy to it. Throughout time, seekers have tried to find that elusive thing called enlightenment. It was considered by some to take many lifetimes of sitting in a cave in contemplation to achieve. If you were persistent and lucky, you would both reach that state and then have it verified by your teacher/master/guru, who was assumed to be in that state him- or herself. That's all different now because humanity is changing, both in consciousness and in scientific awareness, and with that change comes the ability to expand our awareness to greater and greater levels and to adapt to ever more complex life situations. This change comes primarily from evolutionary development and the activation of the prefrontal cortex of the brain, which is a relatively recent addition to the human brain and has been predominantly dormant in humanity until now. This activation causes the relaxing of the lower brain/parietal lobes, the fight-or-flight survival portion of the brain, and shifts control to the higher brain functions of the prefrontal cortex. The key to higher consciousness and awareness, to the steps that lead to enlightenment, is being able to experience life in the present *now* moment, in the silence of present awareness, which for the first time is available to all who choose to get it through the activation of this part of the brain.

So, here's the secret. Enlightenment is simple, yet hard to reach. Enlightenment is a progression and not an end in itself. It is an ever-expanding state of being. To get there, you must quiet the mind, which then allows you to be in a state of calm and peace most of the time. It is a state of *divine neutrality* where you are not imbalanced by the things that come at you day to day. It is a state of *no stress!* Simple enough, right? If you get this and can do this, then you need not read any further, because I can offer you nothing more. If you can understand this but cannot do this, then keep reading, as I will uncover the necessary things that can get you to that point.

In 1908 Albert Einstein's teacher produced a simple diagram of space-time showing the mathematical relationship of the past, the present and the future. Of the wealth of information contained in this diagram, the most striking is that all of the past and all of the future, for each individual, meet and forever meet, at one single point, NOW! Furthermore, the now of each individual is specifically located and will never be found in any other place than here (wherever the observer is at).

Sixty-three years before Ram Dass' great book, *Be Here Now,* established the watchwords of the awareness movement, Herman Minkowski proved that, in physical reality, no choice exists in the matter.[6]

Understanding that we exist *only* in the *now* moment is critical to the process because only in that now moment can enlightenment exist. Otherwise, we are captive to our memories and our wishes. Those memories and wishes will keep us captive to our thoughts of what was and what might be and away from what is in this now moment. This, in turn, leads to the constant flow of thoughts, the chitter-chatter of the mind, which can create all manner of stress that flows from the lower survival brain. In order to understand this better, in the next chapters, I will guide you along a path similar to my own, which ended in a clear understanding of the process and led to the state of enlightenment.

---

[6] *The Dancing Wu Li Masters* by Gary Zukav, page 173

CHAPTER 3

You Are *Not* Your Body!

I have observed that the nature and structure of existence for human beings can be found in the strongest structure in nature, the triangle. This structure is body-mind-spirit/soul/higher self, higher consciousness, or whatever you want to call it. All three aspects are necessary to function on Earth. All are interconnected. All have their "proper" role.

The easiest to understand is the body. Every *body* is born, and it eventually dies. We all have use of a body and drop it upon death. In fact, death is a term describing the cessation of or failure to function of the body. You are not your body. The real irony is that the name we call the body is perceived to be who we are. Someone asks who you are, you answer your name when in fact you should answer "This body is called … (name)." If who you are was, in fact, your body, when the body died, *you* would cease to exist. If you are an atheist, then that is probably what you believe. Anything other than that, and you believe we have a soul/spirit, and in all traditions, this soul is eternal. What happens before birth and after death is a matter of personal belief and beyond the question of attachment to the body addressed here.

This body you are using does have a very specific purpose. Not only is it your vehicle for mobility around the planet, it is your sense mechanism. Sight, smell, hearing, taste, and touch are the five basic senses. Add to that *feeling,* the most important sense, because what you feel in your body is the key to how your inner or ego self is functioning. It is where we feel emotions, pain, and if we are paying attention, energy. It is also where we keep our secrets, our sorrows, the things that remain unfinished in our lives, and the record of all our experiences. I discovered this in a moment of realization one day while getting a massage. Normally, when I am getting a massage, I move my attention with the touch of the therapist because I find when I do that, I can relax the area and receive greater benefit from the work. But sometimes the mind wanders into a semi-dream state, and things pop into awareness. This can be thoughts, it can be images, or both. When this happens, we can do one of two things. We can participate in the daydream as if it were happening again, or we can observe the daydream as if seeing for the first time. I began observing and noticed a pattern. What would occur is someone from my past would pop up in my awareness, and I would recognize this and simply observe what was there. Then, in most instances, I would release and let go of that thing or person or incidence or whatever as a conscious effort and intention. This happened with some regularity over many years as I got my weekly massages to release stress.

One day, the light bulb went on, and I remembered something a previous teacher had said: "We store our incomplete experiences in our body.[7] It dawned on me that when a certain area was touched and an image came to mind, this was where I had stored that person, event, or otherwise incomplete experience. Also, by staying with and seeing the "show" to the end, I was completing the experience and releasing that trapped energy from my body. This only happens when you stay in the observer mode, not seeking to add commentary, judgment, or in any way alter the end result. It is essential only to observe, not change, and this is done in a state of clear awareness. If the mind is allowed to jump in, it will start to explain, justify, modify, or otherwise reshape the experience. This will only serve to add to the energy, instead of eliminating the energy that holds that event present in your body. I know it sounds weird, but it works, and it unburdens you from life events you no longer need to carry with you. This releasing process is actually about observing your thoughts and does not require a physical touch, although it is interesting to see this come up with a massage.

---

[7] Gregge Tiffen, G-Systems, Dallas, TX

So, it should be fairly acceptable for most people to agree that they are only using a body in this life. They did not create it, they did not create the food or air that nourishes it, and at the end of life, all components that make up the physical body return to Mother Earth from whence they came. Dust to dust, and all that.

CHAPTER 4

You Are *Not* Your Mind!

So, we have a body, which is temporary, and we have a soul, which is perpetual. Where does mind come into the equation? Something has to operate the body, which the brain can do without thoughts about how to do it. People in comas still have functioning bodies, right? Science has even said that if you removed the top half of the brain, the body would still function. (There would just be nobody home!) So, brain is the physical component, and *mind* is what? To understand, we need to see that thoughts are how mind expresses itself and look at the nature of thought.

All thoughts come from the thought sphere. The thought sphere is as old as mankind and every single thought of every being that has ever been on this planet, is recorded there and is still there. These thoughts are flowing into you and out of you. What thoughts are flowing inside of you and what thoughts are flowing out depend on many factors.

It's like tuning into a television channel. If you tune into a channel called negative thoughts, you will be getting so many negative thoughts. If you tune into a channel called violent thoughts, you will be getting those thoughts.

> Once you get this insight that you are not your thoughts, and these thoughts are not yours, then strangely you will find that you tune into a channel which is broadcasting silence and you receive that silence.[8]

The point here is that thoughts are drawn into our awareness that keep us focused on something other than the present moment, be it the past or the future. The triggers that create this distraction are the things we need to address to be free of this distraction. What we need to see is our programming and conditioning that set us up for the life we are living.

Consider this: Jung was the first Western researcher to propose the idea that mind is actually a universal pool of thought from which everyone draws into his or her own consciousness and also that there is a limit to what can be held in conscious focal awareness. So, there are two categories of thought, those relating to subconscious/unconscious stored information and the conscious thought, meaning that pertaining to present awareness or that upon which we are currently focused. Those two are actually part of the same level of thought. Add to that the superconscious or higher-conscious thought, which is actually not thought as we perceive it. What most people think is that thoughts coming into their attention and running through their minds are theirs.

---

[8] From an undated Darshan with Sri Bhagavan, founder of Oneness University

They think they thought the thought, as in originating the thought, as in coming from *their* mind rather than *the* mind.

The normal state of awareness of thought is possessive—it is *my* thought that I have. But if we take the time to be aware of our thoughts, we can notice the actual random nature of thought, that is, how thoughts flip through our awareness in an associative manner. One thought triggers another, then another, and so on, ending up in a totally different place than where it began. It is all contextual based on our own personal life experiences.

Sometimes thought is constructive and productive, like when we are organizing a task, planning an event, analyzing something, and so on. Sometimes it is totally off the wall, unrelated to anything, like crazy weird. But most of the time, it is somewhere in between, and we can notice something associative that brought on the thought, which is the nature of mind. We sense something in our field of awareness that triggers a familiarity, associative cognizance. This then brings a string of thoughts, which can be about the past, present, or future, depending upon the context and whether it pertains to our own inner thoughts of self or to those about the outside world. This *something* has an energetic charge that creates an attraction, sort of like a magnet. It pulls in a thought or thought stream that has some degree of attraction, although it need not be an exact match. It follows the Law of Attraction, where "like attracts like," but in the mind, close is all that matters.

Say you are playing the stock market and all of a sudden, your stock behaves in a manner you didn't expect. You become anxious or afraid you are going to lose a lot of your investment. That fear you experience is the same fear experienced by the human running through the jungle ten thousand years ago, being chased by a tiger. That fearful thought could now enter you; it would not be fear of the tiger, but it would be fear of the stock market. But the same fear comes into you like that, and you experience the same emotion. Once you realize your thoughts are not your thoughts by seeing them flow through your awareness, you can then detach from them, and your experience becomes one of reality instead of fear. From that place, you can then make decisions based on facts instead of fear.

How We Become Who We Are

The process begins with the formation of the *self*, that which we refer to as *I*. How do we come to have this notion of ourselves as a singular and separate entity and identity in this world? Understanding this is crucial to understanding how we interact with the world, and this begins at birth. Science tells us we are born not knowing anything, a blank slate, with the only way of experiencing being through feelings. Substantial research in the field of psychology, parapsychology and spirituality exists that there may be more to the story of prebirth knowledge than meets the eye. This includes in-utero experiences, karmic residue, and past-lives carryover. Believing or accepting these notions is neither required nor relevant to the immediate discussion of *how* we become who we are, only as to the *why*. Our physical senses are paramount in this early development process and are singularly our primary method of experience at birth. What this looks like is a process of intense bliss and intense pain, exploring the movement of the body, hunger, and the innate need to be comforted, loved, and touched. Try to imagine feeling your body for the first time. Moving, largely involuntary motions like squeezing your hand, extending your arms and legs, sensing the air temperature, feeling the muscles contract, feeling the pain of hunger and crying out because of it. Hearing a noise rip out of your throat, a cry, not knowing that this is you making that noise. The sense of your mother's touch, the instinct to suckle kicking in and the warm and satisfying flow of nourishing liquid being taken into your body. This is *instinctual* behavior, the desire to exist, to survive, which is governed by the lower instinctual brain.

That is how our programming begins. Day by day, our brains record our experiences. As we become more cognizant of the exterior world, we also begin our conditioning process, behavior modification. This is the creating of the ego-self and the process of learning. It is said in Buddhist and other religious traditions that we have picked or at least agreed to our life circumstance and our parents. Because of this, that learning process follows along a predicted path and is referred to as *programming,* which is subtle tendencies or inclinations toward certain behaviors. What is *good* and what is *bad* is learned, what pleases our parents and what doesn't. This then, in time, extends to siblings and friends, social acquaintances, schoolmates, and society in general. All of these things *condition* the inner self, the ego self, the *I* which is me, whose initial purpose is survival. All of these things create that **"hidden meaning making map."**[9] In time, we forget the circumstances and details of how those decisions, those positions came to be, even while continuing to filter our experiences through them. It's what causes us to make a decision in a particular way regarding our response to both inner and outer stimuli.

Any event can create an attraction in the mind. At an early age, that may look like impressions, rather than clear cognition and thought. However, this does form a basis from which we can build a position or take a stand about something. We decide, "this is the way this is." If I do this, then that happens. Is it good, or is it bad? Once formed, anything

---

[9] First heard in a lecture from Dr. Michael Cotton, author of Source Code Meditation, although he said he was not the originator of the phrase

and everything even remotely related can reinforce that position, so much so that later in life, when the cognitive and thinking functions are well developed, the source of that position may not be easily identified.

Early survival mechanisms probably occur at the time cognition can recognize an outside force or authority that imposes a negative/positive consequence for actions deemed unacceptable or pleasurable. Quite possibly, this is a precursor to that stage of childhood called the terrible twos. It is in that transitional period that the child wholly resists the notion that there is anyone else in the world who deserves any consideration or recognition above or beyond itself. Totally selfish positions are formed, and the ego self solidifies an understanding of how to be, how to function, how to survive in the world, looking at everything it sees filtered through the eyes of survival and the patterns and positions that have been created in support of this. It is here that we form the most subtle and hard-to-uncover beliefs about ourselves. These are called *limiting beliefs*. A limiting belief would be accepting as true something said to you by anyone about yourself, such as you are stupid, you are not pretty, you don't deserve love, no one would marry you, you can't do this or be this, and so on. These types of beliefs are hurtful, mean-spirited, and meant to demean at a time of impressionable vulnerability that forms our view of who we are in the world and who we can become. These views are entirely egocentric unless or until the child matures and accepts a wider worldview. This idea of me/you or we/they maintains a sense of a separate self until and if a higher state of conscious awareness is learned. Those limiting beliefs often hide in our subconscious throughout our lives, shaping who we can or cannot become.

In most people, instinct commands the vessel without question, just like in animals. We support this notion of separation by even giving a name to the body, which becomes the name of the *self*, the name of *I*. The self learns identity and solidifies its singular nature. I saw myself struggling to know what it was that I was supposed to do, how was I supposed to act. When there were so many different inputs trying to gain my attention, so many contradictory behaviors, who was I to please? I look back at my life and I think, *I* did this, and *I* did that. The concept of I is so entrenched that it is hard to think beyond the I. In fact, as one Sutra says, the thinking and the thought are both sides of the same coin, and even our realizations and "truth" about thought and thinking are still the thought and thinking of *mind*. Our concept of the I and the ego self do not and cannot exist outside of mind. The ego self is a creation of mind that allows the mind to hide and act as if it is you yourself who thinks what you think.

This self rarely seeks to exist in a vacuum, so it modifies its positions to fit into social groups but primarily seeks like-positioned individuals to associate with. After all, the mind, above anything else, wants to be right! By being accepted in groups, it satisfies that need and defends the group against those who hold opposing views. Just look at political parties or religious extremists for examples of this. The stronger the self identifies with the position, the less likely it is for that person to change his or her mind. We think that as long as what we think is supported by like-minded thinkers, then our thinking is correct and therefore right. When it comes to physical nature and science, such thinking would be on solid ground. When it comes to philosophy and beliefs, (those things that can be proven only as agreement or notion), the degree of agreement and the numbers of those in agreement is what determines how widespread the belief is considered to be valid. History is full of those kinds of positions. Wars have been fought to enforce or defend a position. Take Hitler's notion of the superiority of the Aryan race, which led to World War II. There is no concrete scientific fact to support the notion of racial superiority, yet we still have those extremists who hold that position. This process can be seen applying to any belief system.

Understanding How the Mind Works [10]

Before we can leave our discussion of the ego-self, we need to understand how the mind manipulates others through ego games.

---

[10] From notes of a class at Oneness University I attended, lecturer Kumarji

These are the six games the ego plays to maintain control, which ensures survival.

1. Domination

We want to be in control, *our* control. This is called domination. There are two kinds of domination. When someone does something we don't like, we punish them until they come back into line. Direct Domination—We raise our voices, use our words, especially trigger words (lazy, trusted you, etc.). We use facial gestures like frowning and rolling of the eyes.

Indirect Domination—We control in the name of love and friendship.

Example: A younger brother finally makes a decision on his own. Older brother says, "It worked out this time, but I only want the best for you, so next time inform me first."

Indirect Domination through skills—Mothers and daughters, "Watch how I do it right …"; Indirect Domination through guilt—suffering, anguish, tears.

Ego always wants to win and cares about nothing else.

A woman asks about her husband's workday when he comes home looking sad.

He doesn't want to talk about it. She keeps badgering him. The situation starts out well intentioned but turns into a power struggle. To the ego, control is more important than relationship.

2. Refusing to Be Dominated

Here, the defender is the aggressor. They don't like to be told, don't like to listen, want it their way.

Examples:

Two entry-level employees, both new, were learning the jobs. One became very skilled and fast and offered to teach the other. The other replied, "I can do it just as well my way."

A wife was worried that it was getting too late to go to the supermarket. Her husband was half on his feet and then grabbed another beer and sat down again, to show that he would go in his own good time.

3. I Am Right and You Are to Blame

Example: A man procrastinated preparing for his flight and was in a rush, packing at the last minute. During his flurry, his wife asked him a question, which he brushed off. He gets to the airport and realizes that he has forgotten his computer and returns home. When his wife asks him why he has returned, he replies, "You disturbed me while I was packing."

4. You Are Wrong

And it is *my* responsibility to inform you of how *wrong* you are!

A man had a business idea that flopped. When confronted with the results, he accused, "You all executed my idea badly!"

5. Survival

Ego is like a bad politician. It wants the limelight and will do anything to be in it!

Ego coopts an idea, calls it *mine,* and fights for it. It uses false humility to regain control (e.g., *She Stoops to Conquer*). It will use ideologies, sports teams, political views, etc. Ego may also deny it is being egoic, but will always justify itself, that what it is doing is absolutely right.

6. Cover-Up/Mask

Used if the first five games don't work or you make a mistake and get caught dead wrong. Philosophize! "In the cosmic view of things, does it *really* matter?"

Rationalize and explain it away.

The Moment We Speak, the Game Is On

We never lose in the game. We are helpless in the game. We destroy relationships and are self-centered in the game. Constant conflict equals energy loss equals suffering. Games prevent us from true learning, which equals a failure of intelligence.

Solution: Watch yourself play the game. Pray we do not destroy our environment through the game, for awareness during the game, and for consciousness after the game.

CHAPTER 5

You *Are* Your Soul, Spirit, Higher Self

Now, the soul, spirit, higher self, or however you choose to describe that aspect of being that is perpetual and exists after the death of the body, is a little more challenging to understand. All civilizations and traditions hold that something remains or exists beyond the death of the body. Ancestors are acknowledged and called upon to help the living, are of concern to the living for their comfort and status after death, and are regularly recalled in the memory of the living left behind. Ancestors are thought by many societies to have an active influence on the lives of the living. In India, there is the story told of two sons who inherited a great deal of wealth and a business from their father upon his death. But after a period of time, they saw a rapid decline in their business and sought help from a mystical person to find out why. They were told they had been disrespectful at the father's funeral and had not carried out some specific traditional rituals and were ungrateful for their inheritance. So, it is said that the father, now in spirit, decided to take their wealth away, and thus began their problems. The solution was for them to complete the rituals and express their gratitude to the father, after which they saw a reversal of their misfortunes. Just an example of the continuity of life.

In some traditions, that's the end of it. One and done, yes afterlife, but no second chances, or third, fourth, fifth, hundredth, thousandth, etc. Think about that; does it really make any sense? Life is such a difficult process, and there is so much to learn and experience. Can we possibly reach perfection in one shot? Can we possibly learn all we need to learn in one lifetime? More on this later.

The Inner Relationship of Body-Mind-Spirit

The body exists, the brain/mind/ego controls it, and the spirit watches. That's how it works for most people. The resulting life is one dictated by one's upbringing and socialization. It is dependent upon the relationships we have and how we perceive the world in relation to ourselves. The biggest variable is the mind. If we see the nature of mind and understand how it works, then we have an opportunity to make things different. Say we read a book that interjects a concept we perceive will change our lives. We decide we want that (always driven by the underlying concept of what is best for our survival), which creates a desire for something we perceive to be good for us. It becomes this inner drive that originates outside of our existing mental concepts and structures that creates the energy and desire for one's life to change. After all, aren't we all seeking happiness? At some point, we perceive that happiness is good for our survival, so we reorganize our thinking to accept new concepts, neatly stacking them into our order of things. It is a dichotomy that mind accepts contradictions that are necessary to change the mind. It is why, in the face of all thought being part of mind, we have teachings that elevate that level of thought and in the process, discard old levels of thought, all in the notion of survival.

My revelation that there is more to life than my current experience began one day as a young man I was walking down the street in front of a local bookstore. A small, thick, yellow-covered paperback jumped forcefully into my awareness. It was called *Autobiography of a Yogi* by Paramahansa Yogananda, and it opened my eyes to the notion of spiritual awareness, of divinity that exceeded my limited Catholic education as a child, to the concept of Maya or illusion and sent me on a path that has led me to where I am today. It is that concept of survival, the nuts and bolts of which are constantly changing and adapting that eventually accepts and embraces the concept of higher self. We realize that we are more than our bodies and our thoughts and that the way we structure our reality is based upon the illusion of certainty about how life is unsupported by anything other than the way we think it is and should be. It is in our struggles and experience that ego self sees itself being better off by accepting and patterning higher spiritual concepts in its search for survival.

Our struggle is to notice the patterns. I think that is where I first entertained the notion that all that was seen was not all that is there. Having developed the habit of observing people and the world within my range of sight as a survival mechanism, I came to first notice the patterns of others, then my own. One must develop a sense of inner integrity to truly look at oneself. Mind is always seeking to shape perception into the box of one's own building, to make it fit to the standards and expectations from which one has built the structure and context of his or her life.

Next, we will look at the two major factors affecting our lives that keep us trapped in suffering.

CHAPTER 6

Stress!

What creates stress? Stress is a state of mental or emotional strain or tension resulting from adverse or very demanding circumstances. Stress always comes from conflict. Conflict is the tension between what you want and what you have. Stress can be slight, or it can be intense. Stress can be an inconvenience, or it can be life-threatening. Fear is the medium in which stress operates. All other negative emotions come out of fear, which is always lower brain based. Somehow, we translate the things we are stressed about to being related to our construct of reality and our survival. It is quite often ego based and, I believe, has that same energy we see in a child going through the terrible twos, I want, I want, I want! Our sense is if we don't get it, we will somehow be damaged. We have built this picture of who we are, and we defend it, sometimes to the death. Often those things we take as necessary for the survival of our image are the very things that lead to our downfall because we will do anything to get them, no matter the consequence. We are tricked by the mind into thinking that things perceived as essential are also beneficial. When the net result of your decisions is stress, are they actually beneficial?

Let's look at some extreme examples to make the point. In some societies, the roles of men and women are strictly defined. In a culture that requires a "macho" image if you are to be a respected male member of that group, sometimes extreme things happen. Say, for instance, you are a member of a street gang, and you are confronted by another street gang where insults are hurled at you. Your required response is to face the confrontation and see who is the superior male. You pull out your pistol and shoot; they do the same. Someone dies, oftentimes a bystander because these individuals can't shoot straight. In any event, the net result is very negative consequences because of the code by which these persons live.

A less extreme and more common scenario might be you grow up in a family that sets high expectations for you and dictates what you are expected to do with your life. They send you to a good school and expect you to do well. During the course of this process, you feel enormous pressure to succeed and please your parents. This stress intensifies as you struggle with your coursework. You worry that you will fail; you worry that you will disappoint. This worry distracts you from being able to concentrate, and things only get worse. To relieve the stress, you go to a frat party, where you get soused, and the next day you are really hung over, which, in the end, only added to the stress.

Maybe you are stuck in a job you really don't like, but you have a family to support and don't see an alternative. Just showing up is a dread, plus your supervisor is an ass. Your daily stress leads to developing an ulcer or cancer or some other health issue because you work in a toxic environment. But what choice do you have? You have to support your family. There are many, many things that create stress in our lives. The only way to counteract stress is to first illuminate the causes of stress and then to face stress head-on and not allow it to be the basis of our lives.

So, here's the deal. We make decisions all our lives about how things are, how they are supposed to be, and what we need to do to be safe and survive. These decisions begin when we are born, continue as we grow up, and form the basis by which we understand life and how we are to live it. There is some degree of universality, but more so than anything, these decisions are based on our family values, our culture, and society and will vary deeply from one society, culture, town, or village to the next. Anytime life's events create conflicts between what is and what we think it is supposed to be, we have stress. In stressful situations, something has to give, because you can't have one thing be two ways. It's hard to change what is, so what has to change is our view about what is or our values about what is. Our perspective and our values are based upon some structure or stand we hold as right for our survival. The best way to get to the source of the conflict is to observe the thoughts that cross our awareness. Only then can we know where to look for the source of our stress. Consider this: if you take a detached look at your thoughts and withhold any judgement on those thoughts, you are going to see what the basis is for the thoughts. If it is a stressful thought or a thought about something that stresses you, the background or basis of that stress will become clear as long as you're willing to tell yourself the truth.

Let me give you an example from my life. In my job as a construction manager, I was required to do a considerable amount of driving from job to job to job during my workday. So, I always had somewhere to get to and wanted that to be as smooth and direct (and sometimes fast) as possible. This would sometimes become frustrating when I was in traffic and there seemed to always be some idiot on a cell phone not paying attention who was right in my way. I would often end up laying on the horn, yelling, or screaming at them (which of course only I could hear), because they were being so inconsiderate by getting in my way and delaying me. The underlying principle here was first that I had a right to proceed in the manner I wanted, and second that my desire was superior to theirs, and they should get out of my way. How dare they get in my way! How dare they be so inconsiderate! The basis for this is the position or stand that we should always be considerate and aware of others. Becoming aware of this process for me resulted in letting go of the notion of superiority and releasing the emotional charge in those situations. This is not to say that all core values are wrong; in fact, most basic values will continue to be beneficial. What needs to be resolved is the stress that is created when we are in conflict with those values.

So, what is the criterion by which we evaluate our positions, stands, structures, values? One of my teachers, Gregge Tiffen of G-Systems International, said that there are really only two commandments: Do not interfere with the free will of another, and do not take your own life. If we evaluate our value system based upon those criteria, anything that benefits us at the expense of another without their consent is not really beneficial. It's the Ten Commandments reduced to the essential ideal. Anything in conflict cannot occur unless one of the parties to the conflict allows it; then there is no conflict. It's the Golden Rule actualized. If that became the norm, there would be no conflict.

CHAPTER 7

Fear

All negativity stems from fear. Fear is what paralyzes us, makes us run, or makes us fight. It is lower brain function that, when not in immediate danger, still prompts survival mechanisms in the form of comparison, judgment, and jealousy, which prompt anxiety and depression. Society forces us into comparison from the time we are small children by parents pointing out the differences in others, whether positive or negative, by peers doing the same, by our schools evaluating and categorizing us by our perceived capabilities. This does not go unnoticed. We are inherently prone to pleasing our parents, our teachers, and our leaders. Social structure sets us up to be classified in the order by which we are successful in achieving its goals. We are rewarded when we do and penalized when we don't. Stress is created when we perceive we need to do more and doubt our abilities to do that. We become anxious at times we perceive are critical or important. We become depressed when we think we cannot or did not meet those goals, goals that are often artificially imposed upon us. We are not allowed to not care or to be indifferent while we are growing up. How this happens sets up our way of perceiving life, what we are *supposed to be and supposed to do*. We are often punished when we do not meet expectations, as if we would intentionally mess up a test or fail to remember the answer to a test question. From the time we are infants and get our hand slapped for touching something that captures our attention and not heeding the warning of our parent, we are taught to learn fear, which gets transferred through subconscious conditioning to everything we do in life. We become trained to always answer to that inner parent. So, fear becomes the number-one enemy of advancing in life and in consciousness. We are constantly challenged to overcome our fears when we are learning new things. When we don't prevail, we set up a memory of that experience, which we store for future reference. This memory, especially when fresh, can replay itself over and over and over in our minds. A review of an unsuccessful experience can be beneficial if the objective is to learn and move on. In the case of traumatic events, these memories are often repressed because the brain/mind, in both the physical (lack of neural pathways) and cognitive (failure to understand) sense, cannot handle and properly process the events and becomes overwhelmed. It is these repressed events and those from which we cannot move on that create the most problems. Even those events without the intense emotional shock of failure or trauma can still be repressed as incomplete events. For example, you're in an unsatisfactory love relationship in which the two of you have grown apart. You break up, but for some reason, you do not fully express yourself, and things are left unsaid that you really feel you should have said, and it bugs you that you didn't. Or you have a confrontation or argument, and afterward you think of all the things you should have said but didn't. Or a plot or scheme you try doesn't work the way you thought (a failure). Or you just wanted to say something but didn't. These are just some examples of incompleteness, and the mind cannot stand incompleteness. It will churn and mull for as long as you allow it; then it will store that incident for next time. If nothing similar pops up in the immediate future, it forgets about it, but it is never really forgotten.

Another characteristic about mind is that it sees everything remotely close to something as that something; it does not require an exact match. Take our dog phobia for example. As a small child, you are scared or even bitten by a big black dog, which imprinted fear and pain in your memory of dogs. So now, every time you see a dog, even a cute, cuddly, white miniature breed, you reexperience that fear, even though the only thing they have in common is that they are both dogs.

Just the thought of that trauma reignites the emotions, the fear, and your body feels those emotions as if they were happening all over again. The reality is that all you have to do is think about dogs, and that memory is triggered. You don't even have to see one. All these examples are stressors, which are small or large shocks to our cognitive system, where we recognize and assign meaning to the events of our life. When these situations arise, if we have not had proper training, we cannot handle the full magnitude of the event, and we shut it down and suppress it.

Imagine if you were a soldier and you were just given a gun and sent into battle with no training. Do you think you would survive? Say you're walking down a familiar, yet somewhat isolated street and a mugger confronts you. Are you going to be calm and cool and know exactly what to do, or are you going to freak out, even if it is only inwardly? Chances are that the average person is going to go into shock because there was no expectation, preparation, or training for this event. Even if you have some training, it may only be to appear calm and be compliant, but inside you're ready to explode. You are being physically endangered, and the survival brain kicks in, leaving no room for rational thinking. Then you will rewind and rerun the experience until you've exhausted it and gotten everything you can from it and let it go, or you bury it only to have it arise the next time you walk down that street or any street that reminds you of it.

What happens when you have an experience that causes you to shut down energetically is an attachment or blockage gets created. When I was studying metaphysics, my teacher called these things *residue*, like leftover energy that is held in the energy body associated with points in the physical body, much like those accessed with acupuncture treatments. I mentioned in an earlier chapter how I became aware of these energy spots. The way they function is like little energy vortices or energy magnets that pulsate and broadcast out into the universe, following the principle of "like attracts like." They attract energy similar to that stored experience, and when something happens in your life similar to that, it pops up for you to look at again. Maybe not exactly, but just like in horseshoes, close is good enough. What this looks like is thoughts popping into your head, triggering a memory. Research has now shown that just the thought of something can bring the same emotional reaction as the original creating event.

Everyone has had thoughts and memories that go around and around in their heads, accompanied by the emotions of the event. The more traumatic, the stronger the response. When these thoughts bring up events that are contradictory to how you think things should be, you start a cycle of reliving, changing the outcome, wishing you had done this or that differently, and on and on. It can literally drive you crazy. This also shows how patterning and conditioning filters our experiences and can give serious insight into why people behave the way they do, especially those who deviate from expected behavior.

CHAPTER 8

The Road to Awakening and Enlightenment

At this point, we should be pretty clear that we are not our body, but we should also understand that the purpose of the body, besides being a vehicle to get around with, is to experience the physical world, to *feel* life. We should also be clear that we are not our mind. We *have* a mind, albeit collective in nature, that has many useful purposes and a few drawbacks. When we access our memories, we recreate any feelings associated with those memories. If they are positive, we feel good. If they are negative, we feel bad. Sometimes we have mixed feelings because something brings a memory that is both happy and sad. We can have any recreation we choose, but choose we must. When we choose the past, we are choosing memories that do not always serve us, and we end up living in the past, whether it's negative or positive. Unfortunately, most memories that continuously pop up are negative in nature because they are the ones that we chose not to completely experience due to the traumatic nature of those events. Our brains just cannot process some events, and they get tucked away to protect us from total meltdown at the time and remain hidden as a repressed memory until triggered back into awareness by some outside event. In these situations, as they are initially occurring, we literally do not have the physical capacity to handle the situation, due to being in extreme fight-or-flight overwhelm. Later, when we see something even remotely close to the same thing, we react again to the memory of the past and act to protect ourselves again, thus extending the memory. It remains to haunt the future, and the only way to clear it out is to reexperience the unfinished part of that past. To see it, to feel it, and then to let it go, to release it. In that way, we are set free and are no longer bound to the past. We are free to be in this now moment, unburdened from our past, which exists only in our memories.

The process for this unburdening is to *see,* to watch what comes up in our thoughts and *to be aware* that we need not react as if it were the past. Science has now shown that simply having the thought carries with it all the emotion of an associated past experience. If we engage with the thought when it comes into our awareness, we then follow the story and react as if it were happening right now. So, the trick is to not get "hooked" by the thought, to recognize that this is the beginning of a story and that we are not compelled to follow it. *Stop* the story before you start retelling the story. See it for what it is, and do not engage it; do not attempt to modify it or judge it. Just see it for what it was, and truly feel the energy of the moment in your body. This requires attention and awareness and a will to be in charge of your mental process. It's quite a simple process, and it's hard to do because of the nature of our memories. Our nature is to shy away from painful situations, and overcoming that tendency requires a warrior mentality, that willingness to proceed, even though it's tough, upsetting, or painful to revisit some memories. Confronting your past might require you to change your positions on some things and will most likely result in you seeing more clearly how you adopted certain positions in your life that are no longer beneficial or even true. Things like thinking you are not worthy of love or other demeaning concepts that are limiting beliefs. This will not kill you and in fact will make you stronger and better off. We must know that we are greater than our past, that we can face it down and neutralize its power over us. That we can overcome. But how?

It has been said that the average person has in excess of sixty thousand thoughts run through his or her head every day. That's a lot of thoughts, even if only half as much were true! The average person considers that those thoughts are their thoughts, that they are generated from their mind. The mind continuously chatters 24/7 because that is the nature of the mind. So how can we change the mind with the mind? We can use our higher self to exert control via the process of awareness. The best way I know to start that process is by meditation. Meditation, simply put, is quiet attention. Meditation does not need to be a complicated process with sounds, mantras, and the like. It simply needs to be coupled with a breathing technique that focuses attention on the breath. (I will provide a simple but effective breathing meditation at the end of the book.) It then becomes possible to separate the attention away from the mind and onto the breath, which then gives our awareness the opportunity to see the thoughts as they arise, ignore the thought stream, and refocus your attention on the breath. With practice, this heightens our ability to recognize when thoughts occur, which then gives us the opportunity to not engage with any particular thought stream and to see it for what it is, experience it fully by not trying to change it in any way, and then to release and let go of the thought. When fully experienced, that thought will never return, and the energy it was holding is released and transformed into higher consciousness.

"The mind is nothing but the flow of thoughts. The only way to become free of the mind is to closely watch it. If you keep watching mind in a very friendly way without judging, condemning or commenting, it soon becomes very weak and slowly becomes quieter."[11]

What you are left with is a still mind, a quiet mind, and peace. That state is called the *now*. When we are in the now, we are present in the moment of creation, where anything is possible, and we are not blocked by our preconceptions and expectations of what can be. There is no stress in the now moment. As human beings, it is our birthright

---

[11] From an undated Darshan with Sri Bhagavan, founder of Oneness University

Blue-Collar Enlightenment

to live a happy, loving, abundant life free of stress, fear, and pain. Who would not want that? The path of enlightenment is to travel in the now. Once you experience this for the first time, you are enlightened. Enlightenment grows as you are able to expand this ability to be in the now, which is characterized by longer and longer periods of silent awareness. As these periods grow, things begin to change. We find ourselves more connected to the flow of life, where things happen with ease and grace more and more. The now is further characterized by synchronicities where things happen out of the blue, as if your wishes are granted without you planning or doing anything, no effort. When we are not blocked by our memories, not restricted by our programing and conditioning, anything is possible. That is how life should be.

The process of enlightenment begins with the recognition that we are not our mind. That point is called awakening. Once awakened, we can expand our awareness and transform our thought process to achieve a still-point mind, which begins the experience of enlightenment. We can never be without the mind, but we can achieve stillness in greater and greater degrees. The goal for most people would be to live with a quiet mind 70 to 80 percent of the time, what is called living in the now. When we live in the now, we experience life as peace, love, joy, bliss, gratitude, and compassion (but mostly as a calm inner presence). We are not knocked off course by the events in our lives because we experience them from a place of quiet awareness; no triggers to negative emotional states are present in us, so no adverse reactions occur. We see the negativity around us from a detached perspective. It's not *our* stuff, it's theirs. The unique thing about experiencing life from the now moment is that we innately know what needs to be done in any given situation because we are not being overwhelmed by our survival mind. We access our higher cognitive processes, which guide us from a different level of consciousness, and we experience knowing that exactly what needs to be done is being done. Life is no longer a state of stress. Life is good! Who wouldn't want that?

One further thing to provide some guidance and direction is knowing the most important starting point for your self-inquiry. The key to resolving all inner conflict is in making right all our relationships, starting with our parents. Because all of our structure started with them, then they are the source of our conflict. It is said that if you have a problem with money, then it is because you have a problem with your relationship with your father. If you have a problem with your mother, you will suffer from needless obstacles interfering with your life.

To understand this, let me share about my relationship with my father. I recognized learning, as with all children, is a process of trial and error. The problem with my father was that errors were not acceptable; the expectation was to do things right, and if not, the consequence was often physical punishment. This created an extreme survival challenge where "I better do it right, or I'll get a beating." His expectation was unrealistic, yet it is easy to see how I would develop a conditioned pattern where I would be highly sensitive to do something right or even be concerned about whether it was being done right, or better yet, perfect. As an adult, this conditioning was then projected into how I saw things not only as a standard for myself but also as an expectation of others. Nothing is ever perfect, so judgment and criticism of the world and others is the suffering state that results from those expectations. This became clear to me when I was operating my business. "Do it right the first time" became my motto and, of course, that rarely happened. It became an issue with employees, and I was forced to step back in my expectations toward them. But I still held the standard for myself until I realized that I was still trying to live my life in a way to please my father! Underlying this pattern was fear. Fear that if I didn't do *everything* right, I would suffer some unpleasant consequence, some punishment. This fear at times leads to paralysis to even attempt to do something new because I don't know if I can do it right. When I saw this, I realized that I had become my father. That realization allowed me to change my thinking, which set me free from the burden of always needing to be perfect. The outward manifestation of this was that my business prospered in a way never before experienced, and my employees enjoyed more job satisfaction, hand in hand, I believe.

CHAPTER 9

Advanced Spiritual Theories

Karma, Inner Integrity, Reincarnation, Coherence, Grace, and Prayer

All that needs to be said has been said. However, if you are curious, the following is presented as a natural next step to understanding some generally accepted basic spiritual concepts. There are those who might read this work who have had more advanced spiritual training and therefore might be critical that it doesn't go far enough, that it is incomplete. Others may read it and want more. I offer the following as a next step in understanding, but please do not consider it complete. There is always more to learn. These are brief and limited discussions that open the door to more in-depth study that is readily available from many sources, especially now that we have the internet.

Karma

Karma is a term familiar to most people. We've heard it spoken in many different contexts, from conversations to the movies, but let's just define it for the record. In its simplest form, it is the law of cause and effect and is an expression of the Newtonian (physics) law that states every action has an equal and opposite reaction. In the karmic sense, that reaction to something you might do is true and certain although not necessarily immediate. Thus, karmic residue or effect can carry forward over times until it is neutralized. My personal take on karma is that it is pending until you take responsibility for the action(s) that created it. I say that because I hold that we are here on this planet to learn and that inner integrity, which is the ability to tell the truth even when it doesn't favor you, is the highest state of learning.

When I was attending a course on this subject and was in meditation/contemplation mode, a realization came into my mind. I attributed it to my higher self showing me that when I came into this life, I was in total experience mode due to the blocking of nearly all previous life information except karma. We are born not knowing anything and without the ability to construct a reality anywhere close to that of the experienced traveler we become as we grow up. Still, certain things in our lives seem to steer us into circumstances and relationships we cannot explain. Now, science and psychology have tried to explain some of this, like how it is we are attracted to certain people or relationships, by saying we imitate our parents. Freud said we are attracted to our mothers' or our fathers' image or likeness, personality, or behaviors, and that is where we seek our mates (an instinctual behavior influenced by hormones?). But think of it, of the seven-plus billion people on the planet, how is it that you find the relationships that you do? Is it just chance, or is there some other factor involved, like karma? This really applies to all circumstances of your life, not to say that fate controls everything, but there is too much coincidence in life for everything to be chance.

Inner Integrity

As I said, inner integrity is the ability and the willingness to tell the truth, even when it's not in your favor to do so. Life is complicated. We at times find ourselves in complicated situations where our desires and actions conflict with other things in life, like laws. As an example, one day I was speeding down Interstate 5 in San Diego in light traffic and got pulled over. I saw the officer sitting up on the street by the entrance ramp before an overcrossing. As I went under the overcrossing, I hit my brakes and slowed down to the limit. He came roaring off the ramp, got behind me, and paced me for a quarter mile and then pulled me over. This was in the middle of the gas crisis, and the state had reduced the speed limit from seventy to fifty-five, a situation with which I did not agree. Most traffic flowed about sixty-five in spite of the restrictions, and I was going slightly more than the flow of traffic, so he knew about how fast I was going. He really didn't have a good case because when he pulled behind me and paced me, I was going the limit. So he said to me, "If you truthfully tell me how fast you were going, I'll let you go." I could have lied or denied that I was speeding, but I decided I would be honest and told him my speed. He said, "Most people lie in spite of my offer. However, I believe you were honest with me. Watch your speed." Then he let me go. This is one instance when being truthful was actually advantageous, even though the downside potential existed that I would get a ticket. Sometimes we have to weigh the circumstances, like when telling a white lie is necessary to avoid hurting someone's feelings.

Inner integrity reaches much further into our souls than we realize. Being untruthful corrupts our character when lying becomes pathological. The most important thing is to always know what the truth really is, even if you don't always speak it. This is because you would not otherwise be able to tell the truth from something you wanted to be true, making clearing the mind an impossible task.

The Case for Reincarnation

I am not going to ask you to *believe* anything I say, only to *allow* for the possibility that this may, in fact, be true. I have always fostered a healthy skeptical nature and never accept anything at face value, so I would not ask any more than that from you.

Consider this: most world traditions (religions) believe reincarnation to be so. Up until the fourth century, even in Christianity there were some segments that taught that this was the case. If you were to study the historical record, you would find references even in the Old Testament to reincarnation. The Bible, as we now know it, which includes both the Old and New Testament, didn't even come into existence as a cohesive document until the fourth century AD and was not fully settled in its present form until about the eighth century. Before then, it was just a multitude of documents written by many different persons at many different times. When the Catholic Church began exerting its power as the "true" representative of Christianity, it threw out all writings that it did not like and created new ones to suit its interpretation of the meaning of the teachings of Christ, thus shaping thought, action, and governance as it saw fit. In so doing, it considered reincarnation to be unsuitable to its philosophy. Besides that, consider this. When I was young, my parents put me into Catholic school because they thought I would get a better education there and because my father was a serious Catholic. In that school, religion was a regular part of the education, as you might expect. Part of that process was a discussion on the nature of God. What are the qualities ascribed to God? They taught us "He" is omnipotent—God is all-powerful without limitations; omniscient—God knows everything; omnipresent—God is present in all places and in all times; immutable—God is all that is and ever was, whole and complete; God is love—this word encapsulates for us His mercy, grace, and loving-kindness; God is merciful—He is forgiving of the frailties of men which, of course, He created in the first place. These are traditional interpretations or definitions attributed to God. So, I ask you, what God possessing all of these qualities would ask us to master the process of achieving an awakened and enlightened consciousness in life *in one shot?* Life is very difficult, and we make mistakes. It takes a long time to learn all there is to learn, which could not possibly be learned in one lifetime. We cannot experience all there is to experience in one lifetime. What God would expect that? Look, it's not my intention to take on the teachings of Christianity, only to show that it is not unreasonable to consider that we get more than one shot at life. Christ ascended and came back. My contention is that he did that to show us it can be done.

Coherence[12]

Recent developments in science have discovered that brain cells occur in both the heart and the gut, and both coordinate with the head brain in the operation of the body (the gut brain) and in the process of synchronicities (the heart brain). This process is called *coherence.* This occurs when the energetic heart center, utilizing the "brain" in the physical heart, synchronizes with the brain in the head. The heart center is our connection with the field of consciousness. When coupled

---

[12] See www.heartmath.com for their studies on heart-brain coherence or Dr. Joe Dispenza/Gregg Braden: Heart and Brain Coherence on youtube.com

with the brain, a harmonic is created that connects us into the infinite field of consciousness, where anything is possible and all creation occurs. When we generate a thought with strong intention or desire and are connected with the field, things happen. When we connect this with the emotion of gratitude, an energy vortex is created that draws to us that which we desire. There is a meditation available on YouTube called "Prethaji & Krishnaji's The Great Soul Sync Meditation,"[13] which is an excellent meditation for manifestation. They also have one on gratitude.

Grace

I would be remiss if I didn't at least touch upon the subject of grace. A very curious thing happens when you meditate. When you expand your awareness, you can sense or feel or see that there is something there not a direct part of you, but somehow there is a connection. When you communicate with that something in the form of prayer or intention or desire, something can happen. When it does, it is because of grace, which is a blessing from the divine. Grace is the free and unmerited favor of God granting your request. In Christianity, it is the granting of salvation. In other traditions, it is the flow of energy that creates change and manifestation, bestows gifts, and grants wishes.

---

[13] Preethaji's and Krishnaji's "The Great Soul Sync Meditation' on youtube.com or Vimeo.com or go to BreathingRoom.com (their website)

Mikal Shumate

How to Pray, or More Correctly, How to Manifest

Prayer is probably the most misunderstood thing in all religious and spiritual practice. Most of the time it more closely resembles wishing: "Dear Lord, please can I have …, Please give me …, Please help me to …" You get the idea. What people do not understand is that we can have anything we want *if* we ask in the right manner. The following is how to ask in the right manner to manifest anything you intend or hold as a heartfelt desire. The first thing you need to understand is that this does not come from the mind; you cannot think a thing into existence. The second thing is that you need to be careful what you ask for. Keep in mind the principles of karma and of noninterference. And thirdly, just because you follow all the steps doesn't mean you are going to get it right away or at all. Timing plays a key role in these things. I once worked with a client who had estranged relationships with her family that she wanted to right. Try as she might, she couldn't make it happen. I took her through a process, and it took about three months for the energy to get everything lined up. Then one day, her sister called out of the blue, and within the next several months, she was able to reconcile with her family, and all was well. But sometimes it is not in your best interests to receive what you ask for, especially if it involves another person. Say for example, you have a crush on another person and your desire is to be involved in a relationship or even marriage with that person. If that is not in their best interest, it's not going to happen. With those understandings, here is the process:

- Sit quietly with your spine erect.
- Begin a calming breath, breathing rhythmically and deeply until you feel settled.
- Bring your attention to your heart center and place your hands on the center of your chest.
- *Feel* the energy of your heart; it will feel warm and glowing like a ball of light.
- Now see or feel in the center of this glowing ball of light the thing that you wish to manifest. Ask that you receive that which is in your highest interest and good.
- See or feel it with as much clarity and detail as you can, the more detailed the better.
- Now express gratitude for receiving this desire or intention as if it was your birthday and you just got what you really wanted as a gift. It is absolutely necessary to feel this gratitude in your body, give thanks for your good fortune.
- Once you feel this, you are done. You must hold as knowing that you will receive this in its own perfect timing, and then you must let go of it, release that energy into the universe for it to attract that to you. Relax your hands and open your eyes.

CHAPTER 10

My Story

In many ways, I have lived an ordinary life in blue-collar trades as a carpenter and then a construction business owner. Yes, I did get a college education along the way, early in the process via the GI Bill, thank you, US Navy. I did spend some time at war in Vietnam, experiencing the loss of fellow servicemen, which had an effect on me, but not nearly as much as on my brother, who was a tank crewman and felt the hot flash of combat with the resulting PTSD before they knew what that was. Ultimately, he couldn't handle it and took his life at the young age of thirty-four. There are many events that have shaped my life. For many, upon looking back, we can see how various seemingly unrelated events have contributed to shaping our life experiences toward a particular direction. These types of events, called *synchronicities,* began for me at an early age and continue through to this day. As I use the that term, it refers to apparent random events that, over time, can be viewed as synchronous toward a goal that is not particularly known at the time. There have been many of these shaping events that led me to the path I now tread.

Mikal Shumate

The first of these things that I remember was when I was about seven years old. My family was getting ready to go to a service at Saint Rita's Catholic Church in San Diego on a Sunday morning. I had put on a brand-new pair of dress-up pants, long-sleeve white shirt, and polished shoes, and as we were leaving, I tripped on something, fell down, and ripped the knee of my pants, bloodying my knee. I was quite clumsy, tall and gangly for my age and probably not paying as close attention as I should have. My father was furious, not just because I ruined a brand-new pair of pants, but also because I couldn't go to church looking like that. What would people think? It was then that I began forming my opinion of the hypocrisy of religion. After all, what kind of a God cared more about how I looked than how I felt inside? What this small event established was a *doubt*. I was educated up to the seventh grade in parochial school, and all along the way, the Catholic doctrine was a part of the curriculum. All along the way, I listened with a skeptical ear. It was during this time that I began developing my inner sense or truth about religious teachings. It would take until I was in college for this to bring fruition to my understanding of organized religion.

I was raised in a home environment with an abusive alcoholic father who struggled with the responsibility of raising a large family, ultimately nine children, of which I was the oldest. I don't think my story is particularly unique, unfortunately. In our society around the mid-twentieth century, not much was known about how to cope with the pressures of survival that came with blue-collar working-class families. As the oldest child, I was the experiment, the great expectation, and the first to disappoint. My father set the bar high, and God help you if you didn't achieve his standard.

During those teenage years I became aware that there was another dimension to consciousness, and another one of those synchronicities happened. We lived in Encinitas, California, home of the Self-Realization Fellowship, founded by Paramahansa Yogananda, the SRF, or as we locals affectionately called it "Swami's." As I have already related, I had been walking along the sidewalk in the downtown area and passed a bookstore. I curiously scanned the display window and was drawn to a particular fat, yellow-covered book entitled *Autobiography of a Yogi* by the same Paramahansa Yogananda. I felt really drawn to see what this was about, so I went into the store and purchased a copy. It is funny how some things just pop out at you in life that end up either focusing you or completely redirecting you on the path of life. This was one of those moments. There were two things in the reading that really stuck with me. One was the concept of *maya,* a Hindu term that means *illusion.* The point was that the reality of life was an illusion, that it was not as it seemed. This is a foundational statement. The second thing was that there was something that was not religion called "spirituality," a way of looking at life that had to do with inner growth and awareness that leads to higher consciousness. I was not particularly drawn to the more religious aspects of the practices ascribed by the SRF, but meditation itself was an interesting idea.

The next thing that happened to change, or more so, direct my life was when I was around nineteen or twenty years old and after I had joined the navy and was home on leave. A neighbor named LaDocia Sheets who was friends with my mother heard I was home and came over to tell me that I really should go see Nancy Tappe, who also worked with my mother at General Atomics at the time. Nancy, she said, was giving "readings" at a hotel room down near the waterfront, and I really should go see her. This was another one of those moments where the power just takes a hold of you, and you feel compelled to do something. So, I did just that, and what happened further directed my life.

I entered a crowded room full of people paying rapt attention to the speaker, a woman about my mother's age, attractive, a ready smile, and with an air of *knowing* about her. She was speaking about auras, or the energy field that she said surrounds every one of us. She perceived (apparently from birth) gradations or vibrations in this field defined by different colors that meant different things depending upon the location in the layering. It was essentially my first psychic reading. She looked up at me as I entered the room. I had not been in the room more than a few minutes before she asked me if she could come to me. I didn't have a clue what she meant, but I said okay, and she started telling me about what I later understood to be aspects of my personality and my predisposition for life. Two significant things she said at that time remained with me throughout my life. One was that as I moved into my career, I should learn to leave work "at the door" because I needed to separate my work life from my personal life. This, I would suggest, is good advice for just about anyone and difficult to do for most. But it did work for me, so much so that when I would tell myself that I needed to make a call or do some work-related thing after I got home, I would often not remember to do it until the next morning!

The second thing she told me that stuck with me was that I would not age like my peers. She said the older I got, the younger I would look relative to my age group, and that has borne itself to be true. As I write this, I am seventy-four years old and am often mistaken for being around fifty-five to sixty years old. There are many reasons for this to be true: my family lineage, my dietary and health practices, and especially the effects of meditation and divine grace. Suffice it to say that this also ignited a slow, simmering curiosity that would take until many years later to blossom.

After leaving the service, I took a few years to figure out what I really wanted to do in life. I eventually completed my high school GED because I had dropped out in tenth grade when I left home and joined the navy. I looked at my life at twenty-three years old and decided to take advantage of the GI Bill benefits I had earned while in the navy and enrolled in college. I also decided that I needed to go to school somewhere away from my home. I had been cast in a certain way by my buddies and friends that would make it hard to break the mold and become someone new, which is what I really felt was needed. So, I fixed up a VW bus to live in and headed north to the Monterey Bay area. I enrolled in the Monterey Peninsula Community College, let my beard and hair grow out, and was able to live that way on the proceeds of my benefits for the next few years. I jammed in as many credits as I could to obtain my AA degree in psychology and then moved on to CSU Sonoma. These were the days of the hippies, so I really wasn't out of place living around the San Francisco Bay area.

During this period, I did a lot of sorting out of what I was and what I wasn't. Having the freedom to learn, both in and out of an institution, allowed me to broaden my perspective on life. College is fundamentally an opportunity to expand one's horizons and experiences, as well as to enrich the mind and learn a skill or profession. For me, it was about organizing my thinking process, enhancing my people skills, and enriching my relationships. I got the opportunity to experience different ways of thinking about God. I learned different ways to meditate and

Blue-Collar Enlightenment

learned yoga practices, while searching to satisfy my curiosity about the true nature of my existence and the dimensions of spirituality. In school I learned about psychology and management. Upon graduation, I returned to my home area of San Diego and began working as a finish carpenter in the construction field. This is how I made my living. After several years, I obtained my general contractor's license and began the operation of several businesses over the next forty-five years. During this time, my curiosity for my other side did not stop.

One day, as I was walking toward Moonlight Beach in Encinitas, California, after having finally found a parking place blocks away, I passed by a small churchy-looking building with a message board out front that said "Chapel of Awareness." It listed service times and said they gave readings to the public at certain times and had classes in the evenings. Bam! Another one of those coincidences/synchronicities? What are the chances that at that particular time I would need to park that far away from the beach that I would have to pass by this particular place and see this info that immediately made my hair stand on end? I was curious yet reserved. I am naturally skeptical. (As a child, I learned that I must be from Missouri, because my motto was always "show me" or more like "prove it, don't just say it.") It took a little nagging on my consciousness to get me to follow up on this curiosity, but I finally did go by there for their Sunday service to see what was happening. (They are still doing this, by the way.) I don't recall if I got a reading or not at that time, but I did witness the process and decided I would like to know more.

I will never forget the evening I showed up to check out the school. I hadn't talked to anyone there about it, so I had no idea what to do or expect or where to go. I walked up to the place, and everything was dark in the "chapel," which was a large room at the top of a flight of stairs. So, nothing happening there. I could see some lights on in a lower section of the building, a sort of basement-looking area, but I couldn't figure where the entrance was. Just as I was about to give up in frustration, a figure came walking up to me and asked if he could help. He said his name was Greg and that he was an instructor there. He stood about five feet eight or nine, had bright-red hair and an afro that would be the envy of most black people, sticking out a good twelve inches off his head. Quite a character to be my introduction into the realm of spiritualism. He showed me the dimly lighted walk, partially obscured by overgrown hedges leading back to a stairway to the basement where classrooms were located. Pretty spooky when the topic at hand is learning how to communicate with spirits! I learned a lot there about myself and their perspective of the world. My curiosity that developed years earlier with Nancy Tappe drew me to this place, where I discovered she was also an instructor.

One of the things I was exposed to prior to finishing college was something called EST, short for Erhard Seminars Training, which later became The Forum or Landmark. My exposure was as EST. This was also a life-changing series of events, as I took many courses after the initial training. What I learned from these courses was how the mind works. To this day, I say that this was an incredibly accurate presentation of the process and that Erhard got it mostly right except for the ending, meaning what happens at the point of enlightenment. Given my ongoing training in spiritualism, I did not have the same view he did.

The next step in my continuing education was meeting a man named Gregge Tiffen. I would describe Gregge as an American mystic, although I doubt he saw himself the same way. He taught metaphysics and the laws of the universe. His readings and courses were all based upon ancient knowledge he received while studying in Tibet. He translated it into mathematical formulas for determining your predispositions to certain influences from the time of birth. It was much like a modern astrological chart but was based on only ten houses instead of twelve. He contended it was much more precise as to the timing of the start of your chart. Gregge's formulas find the best times to do things like initiate a business or the best place to locate or live (kind of like feng shui). His business, G-Systems International, is located in Dallas, Texas, and still offers most services, even though he has since passed away. What I learned from his lectures were universal laws like the Law of Attraction, the Law of Action, the Law of Oneness, and so on, which helped me to understand how and why some of the things occurred in my life, helped me to make sense of why things happened the way they did. Not a be-all, do-all, but certainly a help.

The next life event that shaped my experience was meeting my wife, Kathy. She provided me with two essential interrelated things. The first was her acceptance of those things of interest to me in my personal development, of which some were of no interest to her at all. This acceptance came out of the second contribution to me, which was her unconditional love. Now, this doesn't mean that she liked everything I might do, but it does mean that no matter what I did, she still loves me. That is true to this day, although I must say the evolution of my consciousness has greatly reduced those things that she might not like. When we got married, she had a young daughter, Jaclyn, from a previous marriage. My life changed dramatically with this addition of an instant family, and for the next twenty years, my main focus was my family and career. I now had a family to support. I did not totally abandon my seeker status, but it certainly took a back seat for about the next twenty years until the next step popped up.

In 2008, a good friend and health advisor Nicolai Lennox, DC, said to me he thought that something he and his wife had recently experienced might be of interest to me, being the spiritual person I am. It took several months and several invitations before that familiar yearning again took over and led me to their house to experience Deeksha, or the Oneness Blessing. This, for me, was one of those cathartic, life-changing experiences that opened the door to a wondrous new experience of consciousness. In 2010, I became a oneness trainer. The next year, I experienced awakening. It was the continuing-education opportunities through Oneness University and O&O Academy that helped me further my desire to expand my consciousness and seek to know what enlightenment was and where I found the answer in 2018.

In 2019, a friend introduced me to the Energy Transfer Reset (ETR), a quasi-meditation process that seeks to remove all lower-energy timelines from your energy field that have built up over the many lifetimes you've had, which will accelerate the process of ascension into the fifth dimension of consciousness. This ascension is what has allowed the process of enlightenment to be possible in a very short time. I did the ETR and immediately felt the impact on my consciousness and validated that it worked. I then found out that I was a "starseed" and could become an ETR practitioner. I took the required course and became certified in April of that year. I continue to offer this process to my clients with great success.

On a More Personal Level

I had to overcome the effects of an abusive childhood to get where I am today, one where there was physical abuse until around thirteen years old. Then I grew tall and big enough to look my father in the eye, and I was ready to fight back. One day he was ready to smack me, and I squared off and clenched my fists, having had enough. He backed off and then changed his tactics to psychological abuse until I left home at the age of sixteen. I had to do it to save my sanity and my life. It is a hard thing to be constantly told you are not good enough, that you don't deserve those things that you see your friends have and that you want. Complicating that issue is that I am the oldest of nine children. I know my mother always loved me, but her attention was always on those who needed the care the most. With new babies (nine children in fifteen years) and so many youngsters, as oldest, my role became more of caregiver than child as I grew older. We human beings need love and affection to be expressed to us, just as do our pets. This was illustrated to me when I left for a three-and-a-half-week trip to India, a trip I had planned for years, right after I retired. As my wife works out of town four to five days a week, I had to arrange for a full-time sitter. I engaged some friends who I knew more professionally than domestically who were relocating to another state right after I would return. Their lease unfortunately expired prior to their desired departure date, and they found themselves needing a temporary lodging. Sounded like a perfect match, right? We made the arrangement, they came, I trained them on the necessities of caring for my five dogs, and I went on my trip. When I returned, my dogs had been fed, walked, taken to the groomer, and left otherwise unattended. Their basic survival was met, but these people were not dog people. As such, they had no further interest in interacting with my animals once their basic obligation was satisfied for the day. My dogs looked lost and confused upon my return. They had human interaction only on the few days my wife was home during the week, otherwise nothing. It took me several days to realize just how much they were starved for affection, just like us humans. Without it, we are just lost souls.

I also had to overcome molestation at the age of eleven by a family friend, in a time when such things were not spoken of or reported. Besides, I was so naïve, I really didn't realize the implications until years later. I enlisted in the navy at age seventeen, which gave me some stability but did not lessen the anxiety that raged under the surface. Even though my father was an alcoholic and I really resisted drinking, at some point while in the service, I took to drinking; it lessened the stress. Tobacco was an accepted activity in my family, and I smoked my first cigarette at age twelve. I got out of the service in December 1966, having spent most of the year in Vietnam. I came home weighing 190 pounds, down from 215. Cigarettes were my first big challenge. When I left the service at the end of 1966, the cost of cigarettes when purchased at sea was ten cents a pack, a dollar a carton. Civilians were paying between twenty-five and thirty-five cents a pack, which may seem insignificant today, but back then it was real money when you were making a dollar or a dollar fifty an hour for menial jobs. So, right there was real incentive, especially if you suddenly didn't have a job. What I did was buy a case of cigarettes, forty-eight cartons, and told myself when these are gone, this is it. I was smoking about two packs a day and then started cutting down. As the supply was exhausted, I cut back further and further, until one day in late December, a year after I made my resolution, I woke up one morning and reached for my smokes, only to find that I had only three left. Decision time! Do I buy another pack and continue my addiction, which would now cost me fifty cents a pack, or do I keep my resolution and quit? I said to myself, "Who's in charge here, me or the cigarettes?" I grabbed the pack and threw it into the fireplace, took a deep breath, and moved on, having conquered my first demon. I wouldn't fully realize the significance of this decision until much later in my life.

The childhood friends I hung out with were very into partying, and somewhere along the line, I experimented with drugs, mostly pot, but some psychedelics. Fortunately, I had no real interest in it, although I did smoke pot from time to time through college. I didn't carry the genes to become an alcoholic but didn't completely stop drinking until later in life, when my consciousness was so much higher. Drinking, even a glass of wine, depressed me so much that it was not worth it.

From an early age, I had a curiosity about life, a real wonderment that kept getting beaten down by the circumstances of my life. When I picked up that copy of *Autobiography of a Yogi,* it opened a door that had only been cracked a little prior to that and inserted the notion that there actually was a spiritual path in life. Things could get better; at that time, I had a very bleak outlook on the world. Funny how those things happen just when you need them, if you are paying attention. I did not become an SRF member, and I discovered meditation had its limits when it came to me; why I would discover later. But two significant changes came to me during that time. One was my decision to use my GI Bill to go to college after first getting my GED. The second was to forgive my parents, because they were doing the best they knew how within the circumstances of their lives to raise me. (They divorced within a couple of years after I left home because of how my father treated the children and because he was unfaithful.)

I graduated from college with distinction, with a degree in management and went into the construction business, being more or less successful in the cyclic nature of that business over a period of over forty years. During that time, I nurtured my aesthetic side, becoming a spiritualist minister, by taking the EST training, by studying metaphysics and spirituality under two incredible teachers. Nancy Tappe was the clairvoyant aura reader who opened the world of mysticism to me, and Gregge Tiffen was an American mystic who brought the ancient principles of the East into my awareness in a very American way. Then I found the Khalki phenomenon in India. I undertook a serious study at Oneness University near Chennai, India, where I completed eight levels of training in what was at the time called The Oneness Partners Course, the last of which was done under the auspices of O&O Academy. It was during my seventh level of training that I had my enlightening experience, although I didn't realize it at the time. One day in class, we were given our first exposure to the Great Soul Sync Meditation. This is a really powerful meditation that takes the participant into the unlimited field of consciousness, where anything and everything is possible. During the meditation, you are given an opportunity to ask for any one thing you desire or intend to happen. At the time, I had a massive black, burned area that covered my entire left cheek, caused by my misunderstanding how I was supposed to be using a follow-up medication for a skin cancer procedure I had just prior to traveling to India. So, my intention and desire was that my face heal. Three days later, as the course ended and we were leaving on Saturday night to return home, the black area on my cheek had reduced to the size of a quarter. The following Wednesday, I had an appointment with my dermatologist, and the blackness was all gone. When I told him what I had done with the medication, his remark was that he would have expected to see my exposed cheekbone with all the skin burned off. Instead, what I had, according to him, was skin like that of a new baby, which he said would normalize in about six months. Truly a miracle. Like I said, I did not realize the significance of this event until a few months later. It opened my eyes to what is possible. I have investigated all the world's major religions and found a little something within each one. I have taken a piece from all, and from that, I reached that state of peace within that I offer to you in this work.

I tell all of this so that you can see that in most ways, I am just a regular guy who just happened to be paying attention at the right place and the right time. Through all of these life experiences, I have become aware of a pattern, applicable to all people, that organizes the life experience into a discernable system. When followed, it can bring you to a state of being where life can no longer knock you down. You can experience love and joy in your life, and you can have everything you truly desire. Peace

Website: lovelightconsciousness.com
Email: mikal@lovelightconsciousness.com

Mikal Shumate

Breathing Meditation (Courtesy of Lisa Renee, energeticsynthesis.com)

The purpose of this meditation is to reeducate the autonomic nervous system and balance the sympathetic and parasympathetic nervous system

Mental relaxation technique done daily, three times a day for ten minutes, or twenty minutes once daily

- Lie down or find a comfortable position where you will be undisturbed for the allotted time. Breathe naturally and easily, gradually letting your breaths become deeper and increasingly diaphragmatic. (Low belly filling up deeply, protruding on inhale and emptying upon exhale.)

The goal is to focus on your breath inhale and *feel* the in-breath as cool air inhaling. Follow the stream of breath within your passages and exhale the warm air in out-breaths through the nasal passages. The session goal is to begin a count of a total of 108 breaths, inhale and exhale, and ultimately maintain your focus on your breath without mental chatter disturbance. With consistent practice, one will begin to establish a witness function, where you will be able to watch your emotional life, inner thoughts with much more objectivity and detachment.

- Section your 108 breaths into four counts (quadrants).
- Focus on your breath, inhale and then exhale, count breath 1 and maintain focus through your count. If you find your mind wander, get distracted, or begin inner dialogue, start back to breath count one and maintain as far as you may be focused throughout your breathwork session time. The goal is to ultimately be able to complete the breathwork in one session sequence without needing to recount or restart the session.
- Maintain count and focus through each of the four quadrant sets without starting over, building your endurance and focus throughout the four quadrants to a full 108-breath session without needing to restart the count:
- Breaths 1–27
- Breaths 28–56
- Breaths 57–73
- Breaths 74–108

After mastering this technique, focused or guided meditation and visualization techniques become much easier to achieve.

Alternative Technique

Yogic breathing from *The Hindu-Yogi Science of Breath* by Yogi Ramacharake

The following are instructions for a complete yogic breath.

- Breathing through the nostrils, inhale steadily, first filling the lower part of the lungs, which is accomplished by bringing into play the diaphragm, which descending exerts a gentle pressure on the abdominal organs, pushing forward the front walls of the abdomen.
- Then fill the middle part of the lungs, pushing out the lower ribs, breastbone, and chest.
- Then fill the higher portion of the lungs, protruding the upper chest, thus lifting the chest, including the upper six or even pairs of ribs.

At first reading, it may appear that this breath consists of three distinct movements.

This, however, is not the correct idea. The inhalation is continuous, the entire chest cavity from the lowered diaphragm to the highest point of the chest in the region of the collar bone, being expanded with a uniform movement. Avoid a jerky series of inhalations, and strive to attain a steady, continuous action.

Practice will soon overcome the tendency to divide the inhalation into three movements and will result in a uniform, continuous breath. You will be able to complete the inhalation in a few seconds after a little practice. Exhale quite slowly, holding the chest in a firm position, and drawing the abdomen in a little and lifting it upward as the air leaves the lungs. When the air is entirely exhaled, relax the chest and abdomen. A little practice will render this part of the exercise easy, and the movement, once acquired, will be afterward performed almost automatically.

CPSIA information can be obtained
at www.ICGtesting.com
Printed in the USA
FSHW011532221020
74993FS